DM's DICTIONARY

of

Alternative Management Terms

DM's DICTIONARY

of

Alternative Management Terms

by

Peter Vaux

or

A Sceptic's Thesaurus

containing everything you don't need to know
about Management and much less besides in
short and consistently forgettable phrases

Published by

DM PRODUCTIONS

P.O.Box 218 DISS IP22 1QY United Kingdom

British Library Cataloguing in Publication Data
A Catalogue record of this book is available from
The British Library

ISBN 0 9536161 OX

Cartoon illustrations by Dominic Miéville
Cover design and typeset by Geraldine Florio
Set in Sabon and Frutiger Roman

Printed in Great Britain by
The St Edmundsbury Press Ltd
Bury St Edmunds, Suffolk

In memory of my mother

LUKI

for her wonderful sense of humour
and
ever-present guidance and support

Contents

Acknowledgements

I would like to thank the following for their support in encouraging me to develop this book and for their help in its production.

Richard Wright for his comments and suggestions.

Adrienne Hickey at AMACOM books, New York, for allowing me to quote her. Also Gill Bailey at Piatkus Books and Kathryn Grant at Butterworth Heinneman International for their comments and help.

To Denis Harman at St Edmundsbury Press for helping me through the production process and for being so generous with his time. Geraldine Florio for her dedication and originality in the design of the cover and the typesetting, as well as for her kindness.

A particular note of thanks must go to all those whom I have met and worked with as a consultant, many of whom - from CEO and senior management to all staff (or is it associates!?) - would more than agree with the main thrust of the book, struggling (though often very successfully) as they are with the confusion that many have to face on a day-to-day basis, not least from consultants and certainly jargon. Indeed, this seems to be a fate that afflicts most people. How to make sense of a confused world.

Many other friends and colleagues have given their encouragement.

Last but not least to Pamela for her comments and suggestions, and to Sophie for her presence in the background. They have been invaluable.

Responsibility for the contents of this book remains, of course, entirely my own.

Preface

The idea for a book of this type has been with me for some time. It emerged recently into more concrete form.

The first motive was to amuse and make people laugh, partly because I found myself laughing at so much of the jargon that I, as a consultant, adopted, willingly or not!

Working in business is a fraught and increasingly stressful activity. And yet, most people in it have a wonderful sense of humour, and can see the funny side of the world in which they operate. The higher up the scale you go, of course, the more difficult it is sometimes to see it, or to have the time to indulge it. Certainly it isn't always an advantage to show that you realise how confused it all is. I admire anyone who can perform in this difficult environment.

My second motive was also to inform, at least to offer a new way of looking at things, and perhaps, with luck, help in the process of seeing more clearly.

I am aware that the choice of words has been selective. I know that the balance between attempted humour and more serious content has been a difficult one. I do not claim to have achieved it.

The selection of the words has been largely intuitive. I have concentrated on those words and phrases that have come to me in the writing process, and which have most reflected my own experience. A few have no direct bearing on management, but seemed to be part of the larger picture, and reflected on it, particularly as management terms and phrases now seem to be everywhere, from politics to horticulture.

There are of course many fine management terms and books around, though these are not always the most popular. Increasingly also they have their roots in varied backgrounds.

Jargon has always seemed to me to be a double-edged sword. On the one hand it cuts corners and can offer precise and unique meanings, on the other hand it can be vague, even misleading. Many of the people with whom I have worked share this view. Their presence and implicit support has given me the courage to take this project on.

In my work as a consultant, I felt, and feel this tension much of the time. Whilst we all often claim to use language that is simple and direct, we are often forced to adopt the language of obscurity, indeed sometimes, I am ashamed to say, clients seem willing to pay more for it, and some consultants are happy to charge for it, or so it seems. At another level it may of course be part of the legitimate evolution of language, that both follows and helps generate shifts in use and encourages new words and phrases to emerge.

I have been, some would say, a bit hard on senior people and professionals in my "definitions" here. I know, others would say, not hard enough! This is not done in the spirit of malice. I recognise and appreciate that running a company, even a small one - as I do myself - is a complex business. I know too that such things as measures are indeed important, though so often they seem to be the wrong ones, or are given too much significance.

I know that managing people, let alone understanding them, even less understanding oneself, is perhaps the hardest task of all. I am more than happy to acknowledge the difficult jobs that these and other senior business professionals do. I include good consultants, of which there are many examples, most with a dedication and a sense of responsibility that belies their critics, including this one. Indeed there seems to be a new breed abroad, as the value system changes and the context undergoes a major shift, who may also have a greater sense of humour.

I have also been a bit hard on the assumptions of business and economics.

Nevertheless, it is a trueism to say that the more responsibility and reward you have, the more important it is to be aware of the limits of our status, and of the importance of appropriate humility and of broader responsibility. "Folks is Folks" as a great American author wrote.

If this collection (a small one) can add a bit of humour and passing insight into the harmonious confusion that characterises the contradictions of the world, then it will have achieved its aim. If it has done more than that, it will have more than met its targets!

"But as the world, harmoniously confused"

Pope

Peter Vaux
Suffolk
September 1999

accountancy

The unacceptable face of numeracy that only deals in the past.

achiever

Someone who climbs the slippery slope and manages to stay there enough time to be recognised or think he's important. He may see a little further than others, though that is not a guarantee, and it may be in the wrong direction.

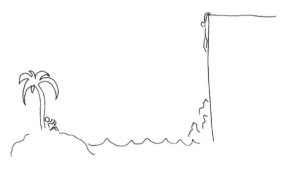

STRUGGLING TO THE TOP

added value

Generally, giving the illusion of providing a little extra something for the benefit of the customer to justify a price hike.

A means of duping the opposition into thinking you're doing something different.

A

agenda

Printed schedule of topics for consideration at a meeting, normally ignored, certainly discussed in a different order and always including items that shouldn't be there. Better used as a firelighter.

agm

Meeting held once a year, for the benefit of shareholders, normally in a place difficult to find or too expensive to enter, at which results and forecasts are outlined, board members are elected, (normally re-elected) and institutional investors dominate. Minor fish can cause a stir and some embarrassment, but are generally drowned out, despite the fact that companies are beginning to take them more seriously, recognising that in the new stakeholding global culture, you can't bamboozle everybody all the time, especially if they own the company.

To be missed at all costs.

alignment

The extent to which people are co-ordinated, facing the same way, working to the same ends, believing in the same principles. An important aspect of a company's culture, and a key component in team-working at all levels. Normally means "buying into" what you don't believe for the sake of keeping the peace or your job.

A

alumnus

Former student of a place, such as a Business School, with a high degree of self-importance, and with an eye to strategic relationships.

Otherwise known as "a lumnus" which is a medieval form of sheet music.

annual report

Public relations document purporting to summarise the previous year's activities and accounts, with a few misleading tips about the future and no bearing on reality.

Contains glossy photos (board members, clean premises, new products); acknowledgement of the great efforts of all staff, and statements about developing people's full potential; enviromental policy statements; remuneration details; names of board members and packages, trading conditions, the excellent health of the company, and lots of funny figures.

Almost as difficult to interpret as to read.

appraisal

A form of assessment sometimes designed to be as positive as possible, which would not be necessary if people were treated like adults in the first place and talked to each other more often and more appropriately.

A

Increasingly 360 degree (that is, being evaluated from all sides, or going round in circles); sometimes 480 degree (including customers and suppliers), and soon to take into account creatures from cyberspace.

B

balance of trade

The difference between the value of a country's exports and the value of its imports, which, in advanced economies - ie economies in an advanced state of decay-tends to be considerable.

bank

Once a high street institution, now a declining trend.

Has no interest in increasing margins and a great respect for the wishes and the needs of customer, as is shown regularly in surveys.

Deals in misery and fictional money which is fortunate as they may soon become cyber-places.

Decline may not be terminal, as people prefer people, despite the margins, and despite the banks.

bar chart

Keeping score on the 19th green.

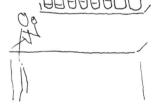

B

benchmarking

Comparing your company with another or other companies according to criteria that are not always very clear (eg Quality, Customer Retention, Support Service, Financial Indicators), in order to position yourself in the market, thereby confusing everybody.

A way of homogenising a sector and failing to offer the differentiation that the customer (in this case people) really wants.

The best way to gain strategic advantage is to concentrate on Unique Selling Points, and set the standards or benchmarks that others will then try to follow.

An even better way is not to tell anybody the secret of your success.

blue-chip company

The Blue Whale of corporate life, but not as beautiful. Large, and visible on the surface. Lives on minnows. Once thought to be in danger of extinction, now making a comeback.

bottom line

The domain of accountants and techno-managers as it is the point beyond which you should not go if you still want to be operational.

B

The point beyond which you will not go in any negotiation. Hence, always negotiable.

The issue is not whether it's important but what affects it, which aren't always purely financial considerations.

bottom-up

In-put from junior staff in ideas, policies and decisions of a corporate nature, normally adjusted by senior management before going back down. Hence viewed with much scepticism. The success of such involvement depends on not raising expectations too high, giving all staff the maximum training and education, and having an environment where such things occur spontaneously.

Less easy in large corporations. Hence the need for selective groups to act as representatives, such as focus groups, or hocus pocus groups. Not to be confused with bottom down which means "where's the nearest loo?"

BPR

Once known as Business Process Re-engineering, which is a grand way of saying changing processes to make them better.

Once a huge industry, based on inadequate premises, in particular that people weren't important. The most important thing was the process. An example of the triumph of thinking over the ability to motivate.

B

It has long been known that the most effective processes can be those that are theoretically "sub-optimal" (not as good as they could be), but work because people are motivated.

In addition to which most business processes ignore thinking processes which are the source of all activity, and should be better understood.

A good example of The Pendulum Theory of Management (see below), as it is now out of fashion again, except as far as Information and Communication Technology (ICT) is concerned. In principle, of course, essential, but not sufficient.

Now known as, "Beyond People's Reach", a subdivision of DTD, or "Doing Things Differently".

brainstorming

A form of group activity in which everybody competes for attention by sitting around a table shouting at each other, whilst pretending to listen carefully to other people's opinion (as in The Houses of Parliament). Designed to generate ideas in the shortest possible time, in which the most expressive dominate at the expense of the most creative, and the best ideas get ignored.

Best done with the maximum silence and time for eliciting latent ideas, unless you're just after a fast-food solution, consistent, reliable and cheap, but with little long-term value.

B

Better to use a fog-horn.

bubble

Something that becomes inflated through excess and expanding air (sometimes hot), tending to burst and leaving the mess for other people to clear up.

Applies to soap powder, stock markets and economies reflecting delusions of grandeur, collective insanity and greed.

Has no bearing at all on current global stocks or the ICT industry, though better to have the cash.

buck-the-trend

"Sod what's normal, do what you think is right."

budget

Imagined costs set against imagined expenditure in such a form as to persuade the board that your ideas are viagrable. A macro-view of cost/benefit analysis with wider application, and less relevance.

business

The life blood of the economy and human activity, (after sex).

1. Buying and selling things.

Views of business can be simplified around two key concepts:

economics or community - ie are you there to make money, or to serve the community? Hence The Third Way, which tries to reconcile the two, which are not really opposites, and bear witness to the mystery of "and". That is, seeing the interconnection between pairs, which form part of the contradiction of life in general.

Soon to be Pendulummed out as the only way, or the fourth or fifth way, depending on how many consultants are advising you.

2. Sub-human activity for economic ends (rare).

business-plan

A fictitious scheme about what you intend to do and how you will do it, designed to create the impression of clear direction and achievable ends, but generally spurious and always bin-able.

Rarely useful except, perhaps, as a theoretical exercise, though necessary to raise finance.

In government circles these are akin to five, sometimes ten year plans, none of which happen, and also make very good firelighters.

business school

A place of learning, where much business gets talked about, and none done. A common phenomenon, though increasingly

B

challenged by technology and other forms of and places for -
well, whatever it is they do.

Provides a range of products and services, including:

degree courses
taylor-made courses
distance learning
in-company programmes
ex-company programmes
short programmes
long programmes
practical programmes
theoretical programmes
fat programmes
thin programmes
and any other programme you can
    imagine or repackage.

The main problem is that they tend to copy each other.
Another expression of globalisation and global culturalism.

Their best selling point is that they increase your
earning power, in direct proportion to your inexperience.

If you want to learn how to act or perform, better to read
Hamlet.

C

call centre

A big place at the end of a telephone connection where lots of young people work on behalf of lots of companies which they know little about (and care less for), to whom the customer is required to call when he has a question, request, complaint etc. Providing desultory service and extreme difficulty of access in the name of improved customer service.

Show-pieces of the new techno-economy.

The best reason for a return to knowing people personally.

case study

An example used in business schools and for company training, taken from a real situation, and used as a key learning tool, in which all the difficult bits are taken out to show how wonderfully things work and to prove a particular thesis.

Alternatively an example where a few of the difficult bits are left in, proving more clearly how wonderful management was.

cash cow

A product that provides a continuous flow of revenue for the company, and that is regularly milked. Not generated by BSI.

C

change

A concept, soon to be Pendulummed, which we all undergo all the time, presented as a revelatory truth. In opposition to "the same", which we all remain at our peril.

The issues are the rate, the purpose, the degree of knowledge about it, and the result, none of which are predictable, unless you are a guru or a consultant (sometimes a CEO, though change is generally recognised first by other staff). It is felt that we are better at it now than we were, at least we talk about it more. The nature of change (eg linear and/or complex) has recently entered the arena, for corporate analysis, planning and activity, and has made things more difficult, if more entertaining.

A conventional opposition is between incremental change (the basis of on-going improvement) and major change (what Andy Groves has described as the 10X factor or a "strategic inflection point"). Both are desirable or inevitable, if working at different times and rates.

Personal change is regarded as a prerequisite for corporate change, though there is no agreement as to whether this causes or follows other change (such as in systems), though clearly they are interconnected. The ability to face, accept and welcome change is regarded by psychologists as important in successful and contented people (contented?), though some would argue whether it is possible to change at all, merely become what is latent in you, which to all intents and

C

purposes is the same thing.

change management

A phrase used by consultants and other disinterested parties (such as CEOs and Directors) to imply a method for reconciling opposites in the evolution of a business, which often means maintaining the status quo while others suffer the consequences. Can be broken down into a number of indiscrete elements, from thinking about it to doing it, though can be couched in phrases like, "awareness", "preparation", "grieving about the past", "consolidation", all of which take time and money, but which are well known in families during the crises of birth and death.

A virtual contradiction in terms, but inevitable and On-Going.

ceo/president

The senior hands-on person in a company, who carries some (but not enough) of the flack when things go wrong and claims most of the credit (and rewards) when they don't.

A maligned position as he (mostly he) is normally the last person to know what's going on, and is generally very lonely and terribly confused, whilst giving the impression of being in complete control.

A position often reached through political acumen, proving the rule that seniority is occasionally in direct proportion to will and ego, (never insensitivity as well), and occasionally in

C

inverse proportion to other people's perception of capability.

Sometimes known as Clever Egocentric Operator.

Also, BEO, Brief Executive Officer, as they pass their sell-by-dates more quickly than they used to - on average less than two years (allegedly).

challenge

1. Any difficulty, however great or small, that can be and will be overcome - or so the hype goes.

Hence nothing is a difficulty or a problem, merely a challenge.

Part of the eternal optimism that characterises the unintegrated person, and that drives wilfulness into a certain achievement.

Hence a significant challenge, is, arguably, a difficult one, whereas a minor challenge means you might overcome it in the end.

2. To be assertive in opposition. A "challenge culture" is the kind of culture that people claim they would like in their Boardrooms (or any other rooms), but few are able to sustain as it normally leaves blood on the carpet, and you can't have too many Captains anyway.

People who challenge are essential catalysts to change, but are

C

only as effective or as influencial as is their relationship to those who don't, just as leaders are dependent on followers.

champion

A person or computer who advocates the change (or other thing that is proposed) with the passion of an evangelist. Hence a culture change programme requires champions, just as it requires jockeys and sceptics. Imagine if everybody was a champion - what then? It would be worse than a political party.

coin

1. a small form of currency, normally in metal, unless it's a Euro.

2. to make up; invent, as in "to coin a phrase". A widespread (and normally unconscious) phenomenon amongst directors, senior management and others (with an eye to their pensions), in order to distract attention from the real issues (which don't exist anyway). The corporate equivalent of being "economical with the truth", which in this case means "being generous with the illusion". The stuff of PR and Spindoctery, the territory of consultants and the play of leaders, particulalrly used in speeches and presentations, and other forms of non-verbal communication.

Widely used by marketing people, designers and other creative phenomena needing to find ways of marketing common sense propositions in the guise of novelty.

C

A huge industry in the evolution of language, as evidenced in computerspeak and global encyclopaediae, and which is one reason why English is so successful.

commercial attaché

Person representing the economic interests of a government in a foreign country with wads in his pocket and intelligence at his finger-tips, who arranges delegations and trade fairs and markets relationships for economic gain. Now, as regulated by performance indicators as most government employees, but not to be confused with spy. Normally immensely clever and once (fairly) well-spoken.

communication

The art of presenting information, of engaging in dialogue, in persuasion and generating ideas for co-ordinated action. Almost always qualitative, and often very bad indeed. Companies should spend as much time as possible in discovering how bad they are at it, and not believe their own hype.

The most important element in business after the product and the customer.

competitive advantage

The Unique Selling Point/s which separates you from your competitors.

Might include such basic things as price differentiation, or

C

product design, but expensive consultants consider it also to be what you do not know, just as they consider learning as including the ability to forget what you already know (and open-mindedness), which, at the extreme is imbecility, or uncontained madness. A good way to develop CA is to develop the potential that lies within both individuals and companies.

competitiveness

A measure of the level of a company's (or country's) ability to compete in the market place, part of the obsession with international and corporate measures and other league tables, which are as misleading as party manifestos, but act as a good cover for the real reasons for success and can be useful catalysts for action. At the macro-level, includes such factors as political stability, infrastructure, legal framework, education and labour costs, at the micro-level includes such things as management and training.

Confused with competition, which is more important.

complexity

An idea that seems to have caught on in the 1990s but emerged in the 1970s out of or into chaos theory. Generally used in opposition to simplicity. The idea being that companies are actually complex systems rather than simple entities and therefore had to be treated as such. A real revelation.

For example, there are all sorts of things happening in a

C

company which cannot be quantified, whose relationships are impossible to define and whose outcomes are unknowable or unknown. Small events can have huge and unpredictable outcomes.

This new way of seeing revealed the intellectual sophistication of the management industry (a sub-section of the leisure industry) for offering another dimension to corporate confusion. What was simple confusion became complex confusion, which led to an exponential hike in fees and enhanced the importance of numinous organisations which found lots of ways of modelling complex systems and opportunities to talk about them.

Also a profound change in the way we think and understand, having a bearing on all disciplines, which are becoming increasingly inter-disciplines, revealing the unity or the relationship between everything. Also, non-linear thinking.

consultant

A person who thrives on offering bad advice to incompetent people, for an outrageous fee. Good at analysis, less good at implementation, often clever. Not always good with people, though improving. A worldwide phenomenon, influencial in all rungs of life, and business.

"of course I can help you Mr President"

C

Generally fashionable and educated, sometimes cultured, if not always cultivated. Often Preppy or Oxbridge, which isn't necessarily a disadvantage, though limits the field somewhat.

Not known for their sense of humour, which is probably unjust, as the industry thrives on turning things on their head (or around).

Occasionally a person with little direct experience who prefers a hands-off approach to everything in order not to take final responsibility or be accountable for anything.

Useful as a cover for bad management and for passing the buck for difficult decisions.

consultancy

A gathering of disparate consultants under the guise of corporate identity, tending to employ bright graduates with no experience and targeting large companies needing common sense advice with a little bit of genuine expertise, (normally available elsewhere) for the higher fees than the already high fees of independents.

Blow with the wind, or create the wind in the first place, by devising ever new ways of saying and doing the same thing, and increasing margins in excess of inflation, and sometimes, like philosophers, first "raising the dust and then pretending they cannot see". Or perhaps, "pretending they can see what is not knowable".

Influencial, sometimes genuinely useful.

continuous improvement

A rather haphazard way of doing things better (rather, trying to do thing better) in a supposedly organised way, following such things as the PDCA cycle, (see below).

Fashionable in the 1980s and 90s.

It can be applied at all levels of a company, from the bottom to the top and sideways and outwards, though normally from the bottom-up, though driven top-down. Requires intensive training in problem identification and solving skills, of various types according to position and responsibility.

Something all good companies have been doing for donkeys' years, though only one of the many things that companies need to be doing simultaneouly. This fact often ignored, as is the piecemeal approach to implementation. Success based on culture, training and commitment.

In reality, discontinuous improvement, as it is necessary to be "doing" occasionally.

C

COQ

Stands for Cost of Quality. A form of analysis that claims to establish the relative value of excess costs resulting from such things as repeat work, duplication, inefficient processes, poor management etc. Now known as COQ-up analysis, a measure of the level of general disorganisation.

corporate HQ

An expensive overhead.

CORPORATE HQ

cost

One of the four key criteria for improvement strategies. The other three being: Quality, Delivery, People.

cost-benefit analysis

A way of evaluating the overall value of investing money, flawed by an overdependence on what is measurable.

C

creativity

1. The principle and action of forming something new. The principle includes conflict (inner and/or outer), though contained; creating the right environment, (for which there is no easy or simple design). Parameters include space and time, and dead-lines, even if self-imposed. The action requires discipline and skill and reduction. It must have an outcome - normally tangible. Attributes include envisaging and spontaneity.

VISION ; SKILL ; WILL ; JUDGEMENT

Essential in all spheres of corporate activity. Evidently so for overt activities such as product innovation, development and design, marketing and customer relations, but incredibly important in human relations and hence management and

C

leadership. Also in such domains as strategy.

Being creative with people is perhaps the greatest form, as it enhances people's capability and self-esteem, in the process of contributing to the wider community through their and the company's success.

Apparently rare, as people tend to categorise it and denigrate it as being either impractical or vague, and is under-recognised. It is the generative source of all growth, and child of the imagination, which is the domain of the "child", an aspect of many adult lives which is denied or ignored.The key issues are to know how and when to tap it, and for what purpose. But it is essential first to know what it is.

One of the greatest means of access to it is through sensitive human relations and interraction, in which people are confident to be themselves, express opinions that may seem unusual or "subversive", but out of which the greatest things may come. Not necessarily synonymous with strong personality expression, as it sometimes flourishes best in reserve and quietness (see also Brainstorming).

2. The ability to draw forth that which is latent.

3. best decribed as a subliminal or sublimated form of love-making.

4. Alternatively banking on The Almighty.

Given that innovation is an essential part of sustainable

C

corporate success, more attention should be given to it on a day- to-day basis.

critical success factors

Criteria regarded as being especially important for the success of a project.

Typical examples might be, the amount saved (cost), number of new ideas generated (suggestions), increase in number of customers retained (customer relations), position in the market (benchmarking).

Better viewed as critical failure factors, as it is easier to learn from what doesn't work than from what does. On the other hand, we all need to celebrate more, especially what we're good or successful at.

Critical success factors for this book are whether it achieves its objectives (see preface), and makes money. What else is new?

culture

Anything from "the way we do things around here" to "the way we don't do things around here".

Includes such things as leadership and management style - from dictatorships (rather megalomania-ships) to co-operatives (The Hippie School of Management - fraught with difficulties). Degree of customer focus, awareness of product

C

and quality, level of training and skill, level of commitment to the community, emphasis on the bottom line and flexibility.

Inevitably involves contradictions, simplified in the (false) distinction between the values of private companies (profit) and those in the public service (waste).

Hence companies in highly competitive environments tend to do a great deal, well and quickly - you would think; whereas government agencies tend to do very little, slowly and badly, which in fact is no longer the case if it ever was, true. Most companies and other entities are a mixture, ie occasionally do things tolerably. The drive for flexibility in the Civil Service is one side of the culture coin (the free market), just as the pressure for increased social responsibility is the other.

Tends to reflect wider culture and society.

However, as government agencies tend to have been sold off or been forced to become more efficient (ie employ more managers and/ or consultants like The BBC - which isn't a government agency) and companies are being driven to take a more "inclusive approach" (ie are being forced to be less efficient), the distinction is blurred. Furthermore, as everyone nowadays does an MBA and reads books on "how to do it" (in former times things came naturally), everybody is now the same anyway.

Once a horticultural term refering to the propagation of potatoes.

C

customer

Person who pays for goods or services. Normally a man or a woman, but occasisonally an aphrodisiac.

The only element in the business process who really matters. The only element in the business that is consistently ignored.

cutting edge

Adjectival phrase denoting "being at the forefront", widely used by conference organisers, consultants and business schools to describe the importance of their claims (and the strength of their PR), normally meaning, "nothing new" or "seen it all before". Sometimes synonymous with innovative, though not so reliable.

Darwin

Known as Charles Darwin, author of the world famous "The Origin of Species". Showed that we weren't all born under a gooseberry bush. Bane of the Catholic establishment.

Coined the phrase "survival of the fittest" meaning, "grab what you can while the going's good and don't worry about anybody else".

Now a management guru by default. "Adaptation", "survival", "strategy", "optimal foraging" and other Darwinian words litter management thought. Backlash possible as part of millenarianism.

He talks a lot about God.

delivery

The second important tenet of improvement strategies (see also cost, quality and people).

The manner and ability to deliver to the customer the number of products at the time they are needed is an ever constant issue in balancing production with placement and sales needs.

An outcome of the desire to reduce costs which led to reduced inventory which in turn led to the development of Just-In-Time delivery, ie small batches on demand.

Being Pendulummed as the increased number of deliveries

raise greater environmental concerns, and also radically changed by ICT.

deployment

The way in which something is put into practice, from policy to quality improvement methods to training.

The two most favoured methods are: by careful planned dissemination through the organisation in a coherent structured way. This is the "classical method" in Total Quality Management, and tends to be "linear". The other is by organic instillation allowing the method and the rate to vary according to the specific needs and activities of different areas of the company or organisation. This is consistent with the idea of a company as a living entity composed of different "cells", adapting to circumstance in a flexible, complex way.

In reality, both methods are needed, though traditionalists and accountants need to be persuaded.

derivative

Financial instrument designed by astrophysicists as a form of anticipatory hedging for investors. Understood by few and an acausal reason for high profile collapses.

development

A generic word that seems to mean anything to anybody. eg, personal development (meaning, getting older), organisational development (meaning expanding too quickly), and career development (meaning, getting the heave-ho).

A word loved by human resource specialists, mentors, shrinks and the rest of the self-help industry, as it is loaded with "meaning", as in "what the hell is it all about?".

In fact, a genuine way of journeying towards self-fulfilment, if your company will hack it, and the best do.

Dickens, Charles

The greatest writer on change in the English language. A Tale of Two Cities and Our Mutual Friend are recommended.

Dickens School of Management, The

A fictional school, but real fellowship, of senior executives who

a) would rather read Dickens than management books,
b) do read Dickens rather than management books, and
c) have read all of Dickens' novels (to become a life-fellow).

And for those not (too) concerned with the bottom line.

Soon to become a real school (in principle).

dollar

Made of paper. Recyclable.

D

downsizing

Making smaller - not by reducing operations or profits, but by laying people off.

Sometimes a euphemism for selling valuable assets that management is incompetent at maximising, more generally selling bad assets that management is incapable of making better.

dysfunctional management

The management equivalent of dysfunctional family, ie in a hell of a mess. Hence rare.

E

e-commerce

business that is conducted in cyberspace. A growing phenomenon, perhaps unlikely to be as big as experts make out as people prefer dealing with people, looking at and handling real products, wandering around shops and generally hating PC screens, and other devices.

But still e-normous.

economics

the study of wealth creation and distribution, based on impractical scientific methods.

emergent

The process of becoming. A key concept in creativity and dialogue. An emergent phenomenon is one which arises out of a context, and that cannot be prescribed or predicted. Important in innovation, problem solving and strategy. Requires skill and sensitivity to identify and encourage.

empowerment

Giving people autonomy so that they can get on with the job and make their own decisions without false monitoring or restriction. Only works when in parallel with proper training, otherwise a bit like chaos theory, without the theory. Subject to The Pendulum Theory and likely to go into reverse sooner than later in some sectors, and in the search for stability, which is going to take some finding.

emu

A bird that runs fast, sticks its head in the sand and bottom in the air. Has no bearing on The European Monetary Union.

environment

Imagine the trees that once existed where the factory sits.

On the other hand, without the factory we might return to barbarism of a different kind.

Can mean anything from "feel" and "context", to "green issues".

Hence "working environment" (a sub-heading for culture).

ethics

See Values.

euro

A currency designed to increase European integration and enhance European competitiveness, likely to increase instability and fragmentation.

E

Europe

A large area of the map at the western end of Asia (more properly, the eastern side of The Atlantic), comprising lots of states (once called nation states, but increasingly a federation of incompatible regions), with huge historical differences - disunited by a common culture.

For political and economic reasons, likes to think of itself as a "power block", thus increasing its leverage.

Rather inward looking and is integrated against the natural geo-position of its various entities.

European Parliament

An experiment in transnational democracy based on anything from 1.5% to about 75% of votes from the electorate who don't even know where it sits, which isn't surprising as it moves around.

An important experiment, otherwise known as the multi-national waffle factory.

God knows what it will be like when there are 25 members.

expert

A person who has strong opinions, the opportunity to air them and an audience who is gullible enough to believe in them.

E

Not to be confused with an authority, who really knows what he/she is talking about, whose opinions are rarely sought and even more rarely listened to.

Authorities are eminent as opposed to experts who are prominent, although some people would argue there are some exceptions who are both. The professional's equivalent of pundit.

F

fact-based management

Management whose decisions are guided by objective and significant (as opposed to meaningful) data, and not on things like intuition, which is often more reliable and cheaper.

Note that 75% of people believe that there is a scientific explanation to everything while 68% of people read the astrology column every week. Another case of a false distinction, and the need for reconciling apparent opposites. Necessary when making cars and spaceships but less so in service industries as people never behave rationally. Sponsored by the spirit of Mr Gradgrind in Dickens' Hard Times, and in strong competition with fiction-based management, which has been around a very long time, and seems likely to dominate.

Not to be confused with management by the seat of your pants.

The Federal Reserve

A big vault in which US collateral is kept. Often empty.

feel-good factor

A phrase used by political anylists which should be more widely used in companies, as it is deeply motivational and improves performance.

fig-leaf analysis

A form of analysis which skirts around the key issues and hides the truth. Common.

fishbone analysis

A common tool in problem solving in which the factors contributing to the achievement of a goal are broken down and displayed as smaller units, each of which can then be analysed and tackled, and collectively contribute to the goal being reached. Also known as the Fishikawa Principle.

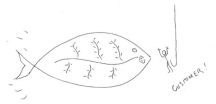

See also Wishbone Analysis.

flexibility

Vital in the world of constant and increasing change, but not at the expense of (fairly) fixed principles and direction (like product or sector), and sometimes a euphemism for not having a clear focus.

As opposed to inflexibility which means you'll probably be all right on the night.

F

flow-chart

Two dimensional representation of the stages of a process showing the key steps, activities, blocks and direction. Essential in process analysis though not much good for complex situations or dynamics which need to be multi-dimensional. Alternative names include, flow diagram, blow chart, flow job.

focus groups

Small groups of people trying to take a photograph of the same thing, but coming up with different images, often blurred.

followership

The up-side of leadership.

forecast

Estimated outcome based on the thorough examination of tea-leaves.

framework

Schematic outline, as in "framework document". This gives the gist but not the substance; the overview, not the detail. Useful for positioning, useless for action. The literary equivalent of "ball-park figure", loved by policians, strategists and scenario thinkers. Almost completely useless.

G

GDP

A measure of a country's total economic output, liberally interpreted as Gross Domestic Product, which, in most cases, refers to a Gradual Decline in Performance, despite the statistics.

going concern

Organisation or business with a good track record, as opposed to a "going, going concern" which is on the way to being a going, going, gone concern. Viable (as opposed to valuable).

governance

The principles by which an entity, in this case company, operates. Hence corporate governance. "You scratch my back and I'll fleece your market share".

guru

Someone who is believed to possess much knowledge and charges inflated fees for telling people what they already know in an apparently new way. Sometimes writes books (more usually has them written for him).

Hindi for teacher.

H

HBR

An entertaining, informative and orignal series of sketches about what makes corporate life tick, packaged in a single glossy volume, also known as The Harvard Business Review. The corporate equivalent of the Comedy Store.

Harvard Business School

Hope for Big Success.

hidden assets

Something that most companies would love but aren't clever enough to possess.

high-flyer

Someone who stands on the seashore and flies a kite high into the clouds in the hope of catching some energy from up there, and getting a lift from the ground. See also Achiever.

how

The most important question to ask as long as it is not divorced from "why?"

human resources

The euphemism used to describe people.

In fact a bottomless seam of potential, never fulfilled and rarely glimpsed, giving the lie to the statements in annual reports about helping people to fulfil it.

Nevertheless a worthy delusion bearing witness to the deeper mystery of which we are all a part and for which we are all seeking guidance and better pay.

I

inclusivity

Once an idea, subsequently a pressure group, now a movement. A way of bringing balanced measures into the corporate scorecard, to take account of "stakeholders", and not just shareholders, in which success is measured not just by the bottom line but also by the company's effect on community, environment, employees, and possibly Martians. Customers and shareholders come at the end of the queue, after senior management.

An approach that has been implicit in good companies for many centuries, that cannot apply to all sectors or all economies equally, and tends to misrepresent the distinction between accountability and responsibility.

Incompatible with an entrepreneurial culture but a lovely idea based on the feeling that companies are simply part of the broader community with broad responsibilities, which of course they are-and should be.

information and communication technology

Systems designed to manage information optimally, which increase coherence, efficiency and the significance of what is kept off it, which is most of what matters.

A form of false God, whose lifeforce is micro-processors and whose doctrine is speed.

Claimed by some to be the greatest revolution since the last one, but nothing like on the scale of inventions at the turn of the 20th century.

innovation

A new way of doing what's been done before, in such a way as to make customers think that it's original, though cutomers can see through it (unless you're in marketing, in which case you must assume they can't). Creativity.

inside-out

Drawing forth what is latent within the intelligence of people "from within", in contrast to imposing ideas from above (top-down") or eliciting them from below ("bottom-up"). Leadership is increasingly regarded as involving the capacity to create the conditions to allow this to happen. An important approach in stratregy and innovation, involving a high degree of intuition and feeling, and access to inner dynamics.

international dialogue

Talking to each other over great distances, with no result in view or intended. A form of diplomacy enacted between important bodies such as governments, global companies, in the constant quest for strategic positioning which precedes attempted or implicit domination. Very important as people stay up all night doing it and it is better than fighting.

issue

Subject of importance about which nobody talks. Hence what

is the key issue facing your company? Don't all speak at once.

investment

> The sound end of speculation.

intellectual property

> The ownership of an idea given substantive form, and the most pervasive growth industry of the first century of the next millenium.

J

jishu kanri

Japanese for self-management, not to be confused with self-abuse.

jock-strap management

Management by the boot-strap, unfortunately still with us.

junkie bond

Addicted to junk bonds, and coming back into fashion. Not to be confused with the Hippie School of Management which isn't coming back into fashion, and isn't likely to.

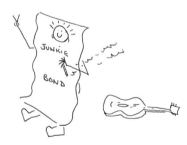

" HEY MAN ! "

K

kaizen

A Japanese word meaning "improve" or "make better" (also "good change"). Led to the fashionable but common sense system of continuous improvement, and virtually the same as TQC (see below). A perennial necessity, not necessarily in Japanese.

knowledge

Mistakenly believed to be synonymous with power, which is a function of will, with some knowledge thrown in.

Real knowledge, so consultants will tell you, is what you don't know. In fact, the most interesting knowledge is in direct inverse proportion to the number of people who have it or know about it.

Cousin of humility, just as pride is the cloak of shame (according to Blake).

The management of knowledge has recently become fashionable.

Soon to be known as "ignorance management".

L

lawyer

Person who gives advice (normally an opinion) about matters of law for high fees. Opinions in France based on principle, in the UK on precedent and in The US on practically anything, most notably the chances of being sued.

leader

Person able to initiate action and co-ordinate others to take action successfully for a common purpose, by proper motivation and due care and attention.

leadership

Paying lip service to the idea of involving people as a means of getting your own way.

A rare phenomemon.

Also a wide ranging and complex mix of principle, motivation, morality and action.

learning organisation

An organisation that makes effective use of its

L

experience, based on the idea that an organisation is an organic form, and therefore needs to adapt to survive, for which learning is a key principle.

liability

Without which there would be no assets.

lifetime employment

Formerly, working hard all your life for the same employer for a gold watch.

Not to be confused with "portfolio working" which means working hard all your life with a plastic brief case and no gold watch.

liquidity ratio

Based on how much there's still left in the bottle.

London Business School

Look for Big Success.

long-term

A time-span of uncertain length, generally somewhere between now and then, (nearer then), used as an excuse for failing to address what needs to be done now.

Hence ailing companies talk of the long-term, as a means of

L

avoiding the failings of the short-term, on which basis they will never reach it.

A never-never land inhabited by consultants and advisers, which has no official or causal connection with the immediate term and only occasionally the medium-term.

The step-cousin of strategic plan, and brother of mission.

M

macro-economics

The framework for trade and economic activity, and the forces that operate within it.

Includes trade and financial regulation, monetary flows, policy agreements and the architecture of the global cottage.

Bears no relation at all to its sibling micro, though frequently impacts badly on him.

Nobody understands it.

manage

1. To cope with; to control; to look after (as in patient or difficult person/situation/or pension fund)

2. To do things in such a way as to create as much chaos as possible, whilst thinking that you are making things better.

Reactive rather than anticipatory, often too late. Hence fire-fighting, or desperately clinging on to prevent disaster whilst actually fuelling it.

management

1. People who manage - ie get paid more for messing things up, and giving others hell for trying to prevent them.

An increasingly large group, gradually infiltrating formerly honourable functions such as supervisors and team-leaders.

Hence almost everybody is now a manager. In other words nobody does anything!

This has led to an exponential growth in publications that serve their apparent interests, a plethora of cosy professional bodies and a certain (though insecure) cudos.

2. A form of intellectual discipline or activity that is pursued by lots of people (approximately 250 million worldwide) based on flawed and contradictory (sometimes unclear) assumptions about economics, business, behaviour, now ubiquitous as part of the worldwide curriculum for everybody.

3. A maligned group of people who run things and normally get sacked when downsizing is in fashion.

manager

An individual who belongs to management, manages, (ie copes) and who has some authority over someone/some people or something, but rarely himself. A sort of cheer-leader for a particular area of company life, around whom workers throng and to whom they do not go when in need of advice.

Based on political acumen and some competence (allegedly).

mba

Master (not mistress) of Business Administration.

A qualification claiming to give intellectual credence to making money, substantiated by the fact that if you have one you'll get paid twice as much as you would otherwise, or deserve to.

An incomprehensible grounding for high-flyers who have not yet taken off, and a necessary condition for becoming important, though not necessarily good. Once a rarity, now ten a penny, soon to be replaced by mbaf: "mind if I borrow a fiver?"

Note the contradiction between "business" and "administration".

mbo

1. Management buy-out.

2. Management By Objectives (as opposed to MBNTTAA which means Management By Not Trying To Achieve Anything at all).

and most commonly

3. "Mind if I Buzz Off?" (see strategic sleep).

measures

Criteria used to quantify performance, rated highly by advocates of success, and without which there wouldn't be any. In danger of ignoring the immeasurable which is sometimes more important, and of focusing on the wrong things and obsuring more important criteria. Originally hard criteria only, claimed to be related to the bottom line, now more inclusive and including soft issues (environment, human and social factors) creating what has become known as a "balanced scorecard". The key questions are: what measures? What balance? Best to balance accepted, commonly used criteria (as in benchmarking) with exclusive and company specific measures which cannot be replicated.

media

The industry dealing in illusions (film, tv, newspaper and other creative expressions) which sometimes reveal deeper truths which are also illusions. Therefore highly revelatory.

A popular domain for insecure fantasists who yearn for a voice and recognition and are often overpaid, but are in many cases skint.

meeting

Experiences at which people sit around a table (normally an impossible shape) in order

The CEO's meeting

1. to drink coffee,

2. to voice their opinions and

3. to ignore other people's.

There are three types of meeting:

> *one*, meetings where nothing is discussed and not much is decided (the hot air meeting);
> *two*, where not much is discussed and a little is decided (the worthy compromise),
> and *three*, where nothing is discussed and a decision is reached (the CEO's meeting).

Sometimes known as corporate seances.

If you want to get anything done, better to eat a fish.

megalomania

Has no bearing on being a CEO.

memo

A message from one or more people in the company to other people in the company, containing very important information about anything from policy changes to product launches to the date of the Christmas Party, which has been cancelled this year, despite protests from staff. This is known as cost-cutting and destroys morale for the sake of a pittance.

Often a way of not communicating face-to-face and therefore avoiding eye contact. Also a way of allowing you to blame someone for not having read it or for having forgotten to bring it to the meeting. Takes various shapes, sizes and colours, and normally has complex reference numbers on it, just to prove how good bureaucracy is. Also used to look serious at meetings, and down at the table while you take your glasses off, which is another way of avoiding eye contact (as well as the issue).

Tone varies from officious (Top-down assertive) to patronising (over friendly comeraderie) sometimes boredoming on the libellous (were it not for the fact that it's internal). A supposedly objective and reliable way of ensuring standard information transfer, though some people think it is better to buy The Sun.

Thought to have disappeared with the advance of the

paperless office (another figment of the imagination) and replaced by electronic communication devices such as intranets, but still with us.

mentor

A cross between a shrink and an adviser, getting a high fee for offering discreet feed-back to senior executives on a one-to one basis, as part of his or her (that is, the mentor's) personal development, and, as they (both of them) are so lonely up there. Highly paid substitute for a friend. If wearing a tie, normally slightly askew, and shoes fairly supple.

Level and quality of advice varies according to planetary activity, like the stock market, though certainly does not effect the level of fee.

A person who listens a lot and can be as critical as he likes without suffering the consequences. In fact, respect is given in direct proportion to the level of criticism offered, showing that CEOs are not the only masochists in corporate life.

Once fashionable, now better to talk to the wife, also now fashionable.

merger

The coming together of two corporations for their mutual benefit (and the supposed benefit of the shareholders) motivated either by the need to increase sales or to cut costs and normally to make money for senior management (those that remain). Of uncertain effect and generated at cosy golf-course cabals.

Almost certain to result in job reductions, allowing staff the opportunity to "exploit other more attractive opportunties in the dynamic environment" in which we all live.

micro-economics

The way things work at a local level, quite separate from and antipathetic to its big brother macro.

micro-chip

A small French fry at the back of your pc, washing machine or camcorder. Needs salt to operate.

micro-soft

A soap powder used for delicate fabrics washed by hand, to give you that extra little something that makes woollen socks bounce (or fly off the line).

millenium

A historical period of some significance, generally 1000 years, releasing shifts in collective interest, perspective, structures and ideas.

A hell of a long time to wait for a party (and even longer to wait for the next one).

mission statement

A brief synopsis of who you, as a company, are, what you will do, and how oustandingly you will serve all stakeholders, from employees to local communities.

Not possessed by many good companies, and certainly possessed by one or two bad ones.

Has the advantage of acting as a rallying cry for staff and customers though frequently flawed by the reality which is often inadequate in direct proportion to the expectations raised.

monopoly

Market dominated by an apparently secure player unwilling to stand aside for more innovative competitors.

motivation

The reasons behind the energy that leads to activity. The source of commitment for the work in hand. Hence a critical factor in business achievement.

Once, it was thought that money had a lot to do with it. One wonders why.

N

needs analysis

A form of questionnaire/research intended to give an objective
basis for establishing a particular need, for example, training.
The beginning of a process that both costs a lot of money and
leads to more being spent (as with delivery analysis, or post
training analysis). Surreptitiously becomes a "want" analysis
if not carefully related to company strategy (difficult as many
don't have them) or specific roles (equally difficult as the fashion for job descriptions is over though may be
Pendulumming). As with all questionnaires, limited by the
quality of a) the questions, b) the answers and c) the analysis,
which allows for considerable inaccuracy, though it can be
done well (allegedly). That is if the company is World Class,
or dominant in the market (occasionally the same thing).

negotiation

A way of attempting to reach agreement for the mutual benefit of the parties concerned in the pursuit of a deal. Anything
from large scale transnational Mergers and Acquisitions to
bilateral and multilateral government interactions or dialogue
(a refinement of discussion with a more explicit intent - ie
none at all).

Otherwise known as ripping the other person off in the guise
of wanting to do business with them, whether it is an
employer negotiating with an employee or a client seeking a
reduction in charges. The deal is what counts, and the clout
that determines it.

N

network

The informal link between people and the ability to utilise it. Formerly known as contacts.

Hence networking, which means going to as many parties as possible, making yourself widely known and desirable and generally parading yourself around. Can be done subtly, where it is often most effective. A sort of implicit politicisation without the politics. Its strength determined by the number and quality of those on it. Maybe the future of corporate structures, the informal binding and flexible contractual relationships between individuals and small groups, known also as the "wired society".

nepotism

An old-fashioned system of favouring friends and relatives for jobs and other luxuries.

Now a way of disguising the same principle by avoiding friends and relatives, thereby choosing the unknown and untried, thus creating the opposite chaos.

Jobs for the persons.

neuro

The energy on which central bankers and high-flyers feed in pursuit of higher margins.

N

neurobiology

Once a specialist branch of science, now essential in business as people begin to realise that developing staff assumes some knowledge of how people operate. How little this is understood is shown in the eerie silence generated when you ask HR specialists what their model is for human potential.

Will form a key component in the competitive advantage of Business Schools, and other higher educational retreats.

Newton

A mathematician, physicist and thinker whose pre-eminence was overshadowed by relativity and quantum physics, and therefore has nothing at all to say to business or about economics. Also wrote volumes about astrology.

ngo

Non-Governmental Organisations.

Never Go Overboard.

nlp

Never Lose Patience.

O

oil

"Have a glass of oil," asked the Minister of the Sheik.

"No," replied the Sheik, "I'd rather have a fixed price or some sun-flower seeds. Alternatively wind energy."

"Happy to provide," replied his interlocutor. "There's plenty of it about."

on-line

Hooking the customer.

on target

Missing the key points.

option

A way of avoiding a decision, as in "one option is...."

A form of liberal prevarication, and the domain of politicians and lawyers.

Otherwise a share option which is popular as a means of involving (or tying) employees (especially senior managers) to the company in the guise of creating a corporate identity and occasionally related to perfomance.

O

organisation chart

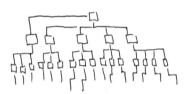

A clear old-fashioned diagram showing who's in charge of who and what in a company, as well as showing people's place in the scheme of things, (and who really does the work).

Now replaced by a disorganisation chart, which shows such things as the lines of communication as opposed to accountability and the relationships rather than the hierarchy.

outputs

The result of whatever goes in, given the mincing treatment of experience.

P

pay

Monetary compensation for work done, or time spent at the office.

pdca

Key stages in the so called continuous improvement process, standing for plan, do, check, act, and an important measure in benchmarking. For example: how many of your staff are doing this?

Each step involves specific skills, though these are normally directed at problem solving as opposed to creative improvements which are as important.

Pendulum Theory of Management, The

A new way of looking at a host of business and management issues (in other words it's been around a long time).

The idea being that things go in sort of cycles or pendulae.

Based on the Aristotelian observation that things go from one extreme to the other, (sometimes here, sometimes there, with a bit in the middle) or as Newton put it later, what goes up, must come down, though in his case mostly down.

Can be applied to everything from inflation and deflation, bank balances, happiness, economies, management fads, the sun, the moon, all forms of duality and subversion.

The real questions are: how big's the swing and where's the central spoke?

performance

The things that you don't do for which you get paid.

Outputs; what you achieve; the goals you reach.

A way of clarifying and defining what doesn't get done, at the expense of giving proper credit for what does.

Something all good sports people, and engine drivers, strive for.

Probably the only thing that matters in the end.

performance indicators

What Auden would have refered to as "ironic points of light" (though sadly without the irony), ie the things which you can see and measure (as opposed to the things you cannot see or measure which are also important).

performance-related pay

A trend that comes in and out of fashion which rewards status more than it deserves, by designing the pay measurement criteria to support the status quo.

Hopelessly flawed, expensive to administer and devisive of all good team-work, if sometimes workable and even partly justified, in some sectors.

people

Widely claimed to be a company's most important asset. Widely recognised to be a company's most expendable. Sometimes referred to as human resources (see above).

pie chart

A diagram in the form of a circle divided into segments to show the relative size of the portions of, for example, the market share by company.

Sometimes known as apple-pie chart which is delicious to eat with custard or a porky pie-chart depending on the accuracy of the information.

P

prioritize

To put things in order of what can be most easily done (the most expedient) which means putting the least important at the top on the basis that, as we can't really deal with the difficult things, we may as well relegate them to the suburbs.

psychometric testing

A rather curious activity in which people are assessed according to a series of complicated, sometimes contradictory multiple choice questions; trickery and other visual and verbal devices, based on the propositions that you are what you answer, irrespective of the fact that you can (and would like to) answer in many different ways at the same time.

An inadequate and reductive form of assessment which excludes complexity, feeling, judgement, and other factors obviously not required. Widely used as objective and trans-national, though Jung, on whose psychology the judgements are frequently based, would be horrified.

eg are you an extrovert with a wobbly sensibility or and introvert with a secret ego? The choice is not yours.

No serious person would claim to use such tests as anything other than a "useful tool" - indeed only one of many tools that could be used to build up the totality of a person's profile.

Q

quality

A word once referring to a product or service of true worth. Hence rare.

Now a grossly overused word meaning a worthless product or disservice resulting from the need to reduce costs, obliterate customer service for no long term purpose to anybody, as part of the ecology of the market place and general economic theory.

Wishful thinking.

cf The Duke of Gloucester's comment in King Lear (the play by Shakespeare):

"The quality of nothing hath not such need to hide itself".

which can be read as

"The quality of nothing should not make itself so visible".

quality circles

Despite being a relic of the nineteen-eighties (70s, 60s, 50s), still the best term for small groups of people (now known as teams) who meet on a regular basis to consider systematically how to improve the quality of a product or service for the benefit of the customer (so the PR goes), often concentrating on small improvements with measurable aims, thereby ignoring the fundamental issues which other people ought to be, but aren't always, addressing. AKA, QIT (Quality Improvement Teams), or LHCATF ("let's have coffee and talk football"), or CTCLGDTW ("cut the crap, let's get down to work"). Works well when people know what they're for, have the time, skills and resources to do something, and managament keep their hands off.

quest

Searching for the unknowable on an On-Going basis, especially a balanced life. Not incompatible with working in a company (reputedly).

regulator

The person or body responsible for monitoring the performance of a particular industry in the best interests of the customer, society and ultimately the industry.

Normally powerless.

research

A vital aspect of any business, perhaps second after making a profit, as it is on this that the quality of everything else depends, though normally it is on this that everything else gets distorted.

Covers such things as internal employee surveys, customer satisfaction, consumer trends, competition, pricing, markets, and product development.

Good research is worth its weight in dollars, bad research worth its weight in euros, which probably gives euros the advantage.

Not to be confused with gathering information, simplifying it, organising and packaging it in order to justify the outcomes you (ie your boss) want.

Nor to be confused with fundamental research which is more interesting and ultimately more practical, despite the fact that nobody can predict what it's for.

R

More should be spent on it, for certain, just as more time should be devoted to doing it better.

A systematic substitute for intuition, which costs less, is sometimes more reliable, if less well understood or developed.

Hence develop intuition.

resources

The potential that is available to you that you may not see, and certainly fail to utilize.

restructure

An important concept for management theory meaning "slashing costs", from selling off assets to giving staff the heave-ho, or "opportunities for development through alternative employment channels". Normally entails increasing costs - at least in the short term - as it requires a lot of effort (more time spent in meetings), consultants' fees, capital expenditure (often ICT) and severance packages, especially if you are a Director.

Includes delayering (reducing the number of grades or levels in the company), which helps improve the status of the less experienced, and puts a great deal of experience and knowledge out to grass.

May improve channels of communication and should improve processes, systems, organisation and plant design, though often a way of replacing one set of egos with another.

retained profits

The bit that's left over and kept in the back pocket and later becomes a hidden asset.

rules of the game

Whose rule, what game?

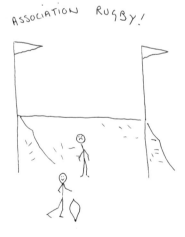

ASSOCIATION   RUGBY!

S

scenario planning

Reducing a range of future options to a reasonable minimum (normally two) and envisioning what they contain and the steps to actualisation. Requires time and a mult-idisciplined approach and is invaluable for government, large corporations and roulette players.

self-management

Getting somebody else to help you manage yourself, or your work.

seminar

An event that people attend in order to get out of the office under the guise of learning something useful (never new), like the cost of coffee.

Alternatively, an educational event normally given by a prominent person (occasionally an expert) about any subject (that has definable "outputs"), of variable length, quality but rarely price. Essential part of networking, self-promotion and tax deductable (allegedly). A growing part of the self-development industry.

short-term

A time-span, between a couple of nanoseconds and forty-two years depending on whether you work on Wall Street, hi-tec companies, or a utility (see below). Alternatively you could be an elephant.

short-termism

A condition which afflicts most companies and governments, whose main symptom is a frenetic response to the immediate without reference to anything other than what people think now. Generally seen in the context of medium-term (one week) to long-term (one month), and consistent with tactical behaviour rather than strategic.

Cynics view short-termism as simply being realistic.

silicon chip

A foolish piece of deception concerning a potato.

silicon valley

A sort of commercial Brigadoon where everything is possible but where nothing visible happens, yet which controls the stock market. Works because of the beautiful sunshine (who wants to live in Tokyo, London or New York?), and because of clusters who communicate informally and like to dominate.

silicon fen

The much smaller UK "equivalent", but cold and damp.

speculation

Throwing money to the wind and expecting a return.

strategic sleep

Snoring for the long-term as opposed to
tactical cat-napping.

A new form of therapy not conducive
to overt productivity.

strategy

A way of making the future happen, which is not easy as
nobody knows what the future will be. In fact a delusion
propagated by thinkers and planners whose schemes like
Hamlet's are often airy nothings, made real by the smell of
loot.

The claim is that those who create the future will be the
winners.

Possibly true except that the future created is not normally, if
ever, the one perceived, and certainly not by the one who
perceives it.

strategic planning

Recognising that "nobody knows anything", let alone how
the unknowable might be achieved.

Increasingly understood as strategic action.

S

strategic thinking

The ability not to pretend to see the future, even less claiming the wisdom to define it, whilst having intuitive insight to an unfolding universe.

statistical process control

A means of analysing variations in output quality to reduce the incidence of errors and faults. As has been shown, variation is much more complex, especially now that the bell-shaped curve is no longer regarded as an accurate measure of frequency at the outer limits.

suggestion system

A systematic way of generating and processing ideas and improvements, once using suggestion boxes now often electronic. Of variable use, depending of the purpose and the reward structure and the capability and motivation of those involved. Although an open house approach to ideas is desirable as a starting point, a formal system is often necessary, especially if the amounts of money involved are significant. A key issue is the ownership of the idea and its commercial value, both for the instigators and the company and how these are reconciled, which they normally aren't.

supply-chain management

Regulation of formal and informal relations between all levels of suppliers and their client manufacturers, based, supposedly, on mutual purpose (a common goal), openness (selective),

S

trust (sub-optimal), shared information, training and mutual support.

In reality a set of highly competitive and dysfunctional relations based on mutual suspicion, cosmetic co-operation and separate agendas.

Once regarded as the key to collective achievement, now confirmed as the source of inflexibility and uncompetitive practice.

SWOT

A form of analysis once based on a company's Strengths, Weaknesses, Opportunities, Threats. Now known as SWOTP, "sorry, we're off to the pub".

system

The way in which something is done (or not done) or operates. Hence very complex and confusing. Knowledge of this is fundamental to any analysis or improvement. "Keep complexity simple" should be the catch phrase.

T

targets

Objectives that are designed to motivate people to perform better (stretch them) and which are often counter-productive. ie sales targets, if badly conceived, sometimes fail to maximise sales.

teams

Groups of people numbering a handful, to a political party, united by a common enemy and disunited by a common goal.

Said to be the key component of corporate life, like human cells within the larger body.

Small groups of people from the same or different work areas often working in competition with other teams within the organisation.

The best work miracles though can burn out and self-destruct.

T

teamworking

Working together for a common goal. Regarded by many as the most important element in the complex muddle that business is.

In reality working alongside each other for individual purposes and gains.

technology

A necessary condition for excellence, except where people are concerned, and of increasing use and importance, and developing at extraordinary rates. To be embraced and celebrated, but placed in context, as increases the need for other elements, other interests. Doesn't help to answer fundamental questions, of a moral or theological kind, though offers ways of seeing which contribute to the basis on which we consider them.

Applied science without feeling.

time management

1. Putting the things you have to do in order of priority and then doing them with the minimum of fuss. For example, put in order:

   a) Driving down the fairway on a sunny afternoon,
   b) meeting with staff re. bonuses,
   c) meeting with customers about a complaint.

2. Arranging your time so as to get everything done, with sufficient flexibility for the unexpected visit to the races.

" WHAT'S THE SCHEDULE, MISS SMITH ? "

top-down

Policies and decisions determined by the CEO and/or directors and imposed on everyone else, sometimes without consultation or in-put from anyone else. Very rare, of course. May be necessary in times of crisis, but normally creates them, and generally undesirable, though someone in the end does have to carry the can, especially those who aren't consulted. One of the advantages of being CEO, or President of The Commission, or any other nominal head.

top-up

Telling God what to do.

total quality control

A system of management, which aims to maximise quality, service to the customer and effectiveness by a comprehensive approach to improvement and integration. That is, everybody is involved in the improvement process (normally about 45%) and all staff are working for each other (sometimes known as internal customers, in fact colleagues), as well as the real customer (neither of which is common).

Spawned such things a cross-functional management, and inter-departmental working (cross-functional teams), in which specific criteria (starting with Quality, Cost, Delivery and People) are established across departments, in advance of other measures specific to each department, both working together. Emphasis on rigorous measures and checks both across and within departments.

The idea is that the machine works best when the parts know what each other is doing and they are all doing it for the same reason, which takes little account of human nature, but is consistent with economic theory.

This led to the idea of seamless government and probably restructuring at the BBC.

Also emphasises systems thinking and fact-based management (see above), building quality "upstream", (though not always inclusive of senior management), and not taking rapids and salmon pools into account. Tends to ignore the human factor, as opposed to people who are also ignored.

A significant movement and approach, ostensibly in the 1970s and 1980s, but also in the 1780s, 1790s, 1830s, in fact,

T

throughout the history of the best businesses, though elements and intepretation change. Hence of perennial value, with variations and add-ons.

Weaknesses cited as inflexibility of approach (too top-down, and too inflexible in application), and of less value in service and creative industries which are more dependent on human capital and expertise.less subject to Pendulumming, more a case of repackaging and retuning elements and priorities, with some important shifts, as now needing to be placed in the context of inclusivity, especially regarding staff and the environment.

Good in theory, piecemeal in practice.

Virtually synonymous with Total Quality Management, and Kaizen (see above).

Otherwise known as thoroughly questionable criteria.

training

Generally part of wider personal development (getting older) and including such skills as maintenance; improvement; communication; motivation; technical skills; leadership/ followership.

Undoubtedly best when rigorous, specific, systematic and measured as long as there is room for the development of more open-ended forms of creativity and expression, given the importance of innovation at all levels of a company.

Alternatively, preparing people to do something that they could have done on their own whilst making it more difficult and full of jargon, though contributing to their marketability and status, justifying more pay.

A way of giving employment to those people who tend to be less able to "do", than those who wish to be better at doing, thereby a form of double negative in which incompetence is multiplied.

U

United Nations

A very large group of nations (many of them internally disunited) with a confused remit and too few resources. Doing its best under impossible circumstances and in need of more credibility, and reform. The political counterbalance to national sovereignty and military power.

United States of America

The land of dreams, where the reality belies the image more than the image does justice to its real wealth. The most productive country in the world and the most powerful and dynamic economy, thriving on debt trade imbalance. Also the most important market for business books.

user-friendly

A marketing term for difficult to use. Manuals and instructions are invariably user-friendly, meaning incredibly difficult to read, let alone understand, just as the product is not often designed with the customer in mind. Why is it that plastic cups used for hot drinks have no effective cover on them and invariably burn you?

utility

A leviathan entity, large and desperately slow, supplying basic products or services such as Water and Electricity. Regarded as strategically important and therefore subject to stricter controls, hence all the takeovers (by the French).

U

As opposed to an inutility which supplies superfluous products and services, ie everything else.

V

values

The principles which we know to be true and in which we believe, but by which we don't always operate, usually presented as integrity. These inform and guide behaviour and business, like how do we act responsibly to all entities whilst increasing margins, screwing the customer and driving competitors off the map. Seriously, though, it is possible to have integrity and be in business, be responsible and succeed, as long as we maintain the right to do things differently when we're "up against it".

Companies that are "values" driven, it has been shown, tend to be more successful in the long term, though it cannot be easy in fast moving, highly competitive environments.

In essence, the guiding light that shines through the best companies (as it does with the best people), and has done for hundreds of years, which balances economic criteria with commitment to staff and the wider community. As formulated by The Caux Principles.

An incredibly beautiful and difficult dance, that reconciles opposites and pays homage to disparate influences.

vertical integration

A gardening term synonymous with wooden trellises on which flowers and beans grow. The point is that all elements in the production chain, namely the earth, the plant itself and the beans, are interconnected, creating a stronger (and less

V

flexible) entity. Often contrasted with horizontal integration which is what most people try to do on a Saturday night.

virtual company

A company with no physical base either operating in cyber-space or by disparate small entities. Soon to have no products, no staff and no purpose apart from making virtual money.

W

Wall Street

A treeless avenue in New York where dreams are lost and made, and then lost again. Symbolic of dynamic animalism, or dianymism, and based on largely fictional assets, but a great place to be and full of energy.

Not to be confused with tree street, where the energy's lush.

webworking

Networking in cyberspace.

wishbone analysis

Advanced form of problem solving, linked to scenario planning as has only two options and one solution. Based on a wish and a chicken. Only works if the bone is dry and if you win.

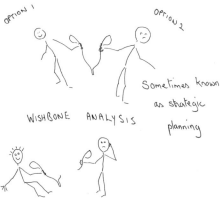

W

work

Occupation for unproductive ends and for too little pay.

What else is there to do?

workaholic

Someone who works excessively, or who prefers work to alcohol.

A person who has no balance in his life, putting work above everything else and who does not realise that life, in all its aspects, is the work, not work itself. Regarded as a compliment in some circles, where status and material or professional achievement are the only measures of success. People likely to be obsessive in other ways, and not very nice. But as the world speeds up and competition increases and standards become more global, the pressures and their numbers are likely to increase.

world class

Achieving the highest standards of corporate .xcellence (see below), once based on purely economic but now with more inclusive factors (see "inclusivity" above). As opposed to continental or nation class which sounds more tawdry.

World Trade Organisation

International Body with lots of members - except China (who only represent c 21.02653 % of the world's population) -

W

whose aim is to facilitate open trade and resolve international trade disputes.

In fact a form of lobby, manipulated by the most powerful at the expense of the most noble, leading to decisions which favour the strong. In the process of being restructured and soon to be redeployed.

world-wide web

The ever-expanding, increasingly rapid and ubiquitous, interconnected group of smaller communication networks - the nervous system of worldwide relatedness: making everybody accessible to everybody else, in theory. Controlled by a worldwide spider, made up of the telecommunications, satellite and software companies.

Impossible to get off it once on, unless you're a wasp.

Soon to become the galactic web, or universal web, with direct access to The Almighty.

X

.xcellence

Quality measured with varying degrees presicion, by such prizes as The Deming Prize in Japan, The Baldridge Award in The United States and The European Quality Award in Europe, also capable of being expressed in being "World Class", and other benchmarks.

The Search for it energised the market for management books and other fiction, as well as the insights, and unleashed the popularisation and simplification of difficult work, leading to greater claims and expectations by consultants and clients alike.

True Perfection (rather higher in every sense than .xcellence) is of course of the life, not of the work, though the work isn't a bad starting point, and easier. Nor a belly full of laughs either.

Y

yen

An intercontinental currency. A mix of the yin and the yan, with a touch of the zen. Also a Japanese preserve.

yo-yo

A game played by children from six upwards (they're too short otherwise) in which a circular object dangles on a string which goes up and down, sometimes at will (a bit like horizontal integration).

Has no bearing on the mood swings of Chief Executive Officers.

Something that Father Christmas says when he goes down chimneys in Japan.

Z

zeitgeist

German word used by historians and social scientists understood as "the spirit of the age", something that goes deeper than marketing or product development and is intangible but manifest in movements, collective interests and shifts in consciousness and perhaps, behaviour.

An elusive element in our collective psyche which begs attention and requires solace, often expressed in transnational and transcultural trends. Consistent with millenarianism.

Something that all businesses should be aware off, and increasingly are (allegedly), as it impacts on their identity, policies, ability to attract and retain staff, products, strategies, role. Hence environmental issues, issues of corporate government and of responsibilities, are more than fads or fashions but expressions of deeper, more long-lasting concerns, about the nature, purpose and responsibilities of companies, indeed all of us.

Examples are: green investment; collective anxiety; football, micro-chips and internetitis.

The explosion in ICT has a correspondence with an inner underlying unity between peoples which may lead to ever-increasing co-operation and mutual understanding, and a more effective UNO.

Z

zero defects

Part of Total Quality Management in which manufacturers aim to produce 100% perfect products, thus enabling minimal checking, increased customer loyalty, reduced costs.

Gained prominence when manufacturers realised that producing faulty goods was wasteful and not conducive to good customer or supplier relations.

A worthy, if sometimes misguided aim, as it has been shown that people under pressure to reduce errors often actually produce more, thus proving the inverse rule that the more you try to do something the more likely the opposite will happen, sometimes known as z...d's law.

Not conducive to learning as it is only through mistakes that learning occurs (apparently).

zoo

A place where different wild animals are kept so that people can see them.

Company: a place where tame animals are kept so that people can control them.

About the author

Peter Vaux is a consultant and a writer. As a consultant he specialises in what is known in the industry as change management, improvement strategies and culture change, all of which basicaly means how to make things better than they are now. His success rate is variable, as are his fees, but more than 75% (according to him), and a little bit more than that according to his clients. He also works as an adviser to Chief Executives and directors, with a special emphasis on personal change. He has spoken at corporate conferences across the UK and has lectured widely, including to The Institute of Directors and The Institute of Management. He has trained managers from 21 countries, and has written a book on On-Going Improvement. He has a special interest in creativity.

He read English at Oxford as a first degree, did research in Zoology, then a PGCE. He taught for several years in London before setting up his own consultancy.

He also has his own company, with varied interests from publishing to film development.

As a writer he has written a novel, short stories, and screenplays. Born in New York, he now lives in Suffolk, England.

DM'S DICTIONARY
of Alternative Management Terms
is available from the publisher.
To order, please fill in the form below and post it to:-
DM Productions, P.O. Box 218, Diss, IP22 1QY United Kingdom

Yes, please send me _____ copies of *DM's Dictionary of Alternative Management Terms* @ £6.99 per copy. Please add £1.00 per copy for postage and packaging within the UK for the first copy and 25p for subsequent copies. Overseas orders, please add £2.95 service charge.

Name _____

Address _____

_____

Postcode _____ Country _____

Number of copies required _____ Total Value of order _____

Please send a cheque or postal order made payable to DM Productions to the above address.

Books will be sent by surface mail, but quotes for airmail despatches will be given on request.

For telephone orders, please contact + 44 (0) 1359 251206 during normal office hours (with a 24-hour answering service).

For orders by fax contact + 44 (0) 1359 251092

Names and addresses will remain confidential to the publishers.

☐ Please tick if you would like to be sent details of further DM Productions' publications.